Understanding Corporate America

Dynamic Software Solutions

© Herman R. Willett

http://www.lulu.com/hrwillett/

Published by: Herman R. Willett

Understanding Corporate America

Published by Lulu

ISBN: 978-1-105-62439-1

First Edition: December 2002
Revised Edition: August 2011
Revised Edition: October 2011

ISBN 978-1-105-62439-1

90000

9 781105 624391

Understanding Corporate America
© Herman R. Willett

Printed in the United States of America

DISCLAIMER

This book is based upon real live events of the author and the education it gave him on how Corporate America operates. While this may not be correct for all corporations, it is to be taken as an educational guide to understanding how corporate America works and especially in modern times when profit is more important than ethics and peoples lives and families.

The actual locations of the events have been given different names and the people involved other than the author have been given new names in the text in order to protect their identity as some still work for the companies involved.

Understanding Corporate America

© Herman R. Willett

Understanding Corporate America
© Herman R. Willett

Table of Consents

Understanding Corporate America

Understanding Corporate America
© Herman R. Willett

About the Author

Herman Rouge Willett was born the sun of Herman Jackson Willett and Tinnie Wayne Lawson on December 14, 1960 in the town of Cleveland Texas, the first of 4 children.

At the age of 4, Herman became interested in science due to events in his life and then at ate 10 started playing with electronics and by age 14 had built his first computer from scratch, including the operating system, circuit bards, etc. By age 15 he had a very good company, Willie Digits, eventually he renamed it to Dynamic Software Solutions as well as getting his ham radio license, KA5NHE in 1978.

In 1978 Herman went to work for an electrical company in Liberty, TX as an apprentice electrician, and within a year had got his Masters Electrician license age 19.

During this period of time Herman worked not only as an oil field electrician, but also worked for a phone company, a off shore underwater cable splicing service, police monitoring and tracking systems, and software engineering companies until he was hired by one of the major oil companies that he was working for as a contract electrician at the time because he solved a 3 year old problem in 3 days that has dumbfounded may engineers and programmers.

At this point Herman was practically hired on the spot and eventually put in charge of the Cyber Systems Engineering division for the new cyber systems division of the refinery modernization.

Over time he created several new systems that confused the professional and corporate level people as how they worked. Additionally during this time he almost got himself fired many times due to not knowing when to keep his mouth shout, but in the end this open mouth got him promotion up the chain to corporate level and a new education process started.

This book is about the years of lessons learned that in today's world would most likely get the best people fired and the lower qualified people promoted.

This concept will be explained in detail through out the book and covered again in detail in the final chapter.

© Herman R. Willett

Willie Digits

In 1974 Herman built his first fully functional computer from scratch for his 8th grade science fair and got 2nd place in the local school but 1st place in county. This moved him forward to the geek status.

In 1974 Herman started Willie Digits in which he worked on building small electronic devices, Citizen Band Radios as well as oil field monitoring systems as his dad worked in the oil field and needed ways to help monitor things without having to drive to them constantly all night long.

Building all this equipment from scratch from experimenting and reading text books helped start the education that the schools did not provide at the time and eventually Willie Digits became a big success in the early computer, electronics and CB Radio error of the late 70's. Then the TRS80 came about and things went down hill for Willie Digits, however new things were needed, Software, so Willie Digits became Dynamic Software Solutions, or Dynasoft.

Understanding Corporate America
© Herman R. Willett

Dynamic Software Solutions

Dynamic Software Solutions started building software to be used on the TRS80 machines in Liberty County Texas, mostly co-workers and school friends.

However during the oil field crash of the early 80's when Herman had to work for an independent phone company that put in pay phones, he developed software that monitored the pay phones and knew when they were getting full of monody so that some one could be sent out to empty them before they became to fool.

This was a major income for the Willett Family during this period of time up until 1976 when Herman was called back to the electrical company to take over a supervisory position for electricians working in several of the local refineries as they were upgrading their systems to new electronic and electrical functionalities.

At this point Dynasoft was put down but still active as the income from working in the oil fields was better and the family needed the income.

Understanding Corporate America

Becoming and Electrician

When Herman became an electrician it was due to the good pay and years of electrical experience. However this is also where some of the first hard lessons were learned, especially one that was ignored for many years, to keep his mouth shut.

After about a month on the job, the first big lesson that took place and which Herman practically ignored as well as learned from took place.

Herman and the old electrician who had been on the job for some 30 years went out on a mission to install a three-phase motor on a gas pump in the oil fields in south Texas. This one had a flow rate detector for the current flow that would shut it down if it detected any problems, neither Herman nor the other experience electrician had ever hooked one up before, but since they both had worked with three phase systems before, it seemed to be a simple issue.

While doing the installation, Herman noticed that the experienced electrician was making a major mistake and pointed it out to him.

He told Herman to shut up and pay attention and learn. Herman again pointed out the mistake and was told to go get in the electrician's truck.

Herman did so gratefully as he did not want to be near the system when it was powered up. While sitting in the truck Herman watched the other electrician wire things up and was glad that he was not going to be near the system when it was powered up with the three-phase feed.

Finally the other electrician finished up the installation and turned on the power and blew the breakers feeding the system instantly. He replaced the breakers and did the same thing and they blew again.

The electrician then called for Herman to come and help him removed the system to take back to the shop because it was defective. Herman helped him load it on the truck and take it back to the shop.

While he was in the office explaining to the boss that they new system installed was defective, Herman took it to the back testing facility and connected it up correctly and started it up.

Understanding Corporate America

When the electrician and the boss and supervisor walked in and saw it running they asked what Herman did to fix it, he simply said, "I just wired it correctly like I tried to explain to 'him' when we were out there but he refused."

The other electrician became a big enemy of Herman but the company owner and the supervisor took a new approach to Herman.

Understanding Corporate America
© Herman R. Willett

© Herman R. Willett

Returning to Software Development

When the oil field crashed in 1983 and all the oil field installations had to be undone, work for oil field electricians became almost non-existent by 1984.

At this time Herman went back into software development when he went to work for a phone company (mentioned earlier). It was during this time that he made a living doing phone installations as well as developing software for the pay phone monitoring systems he created for the new company.

During this time things changed a lot, not only were software being built for this company but for many others who were coming into the digital age and new lessons were learned but ignored again.

In 1986, Herman was out on a job working with phone installations when he saw some people with another company installing some cabling and noticed a big mistake. He stopped what he was doing and pointed out the mistake.

The electricians said it met the National Electrical Code standards, which Herman agreed that it did, but still there was a physical issue based on the physical sciences involved in the installation. This completely confused the electricians and made them really mad.

Herman continued to point things out to them but they ignored him and completed the installation based upon the engineering standards and directives of the National Electrical Code. And when the system was implemented a week or so later everything Herman said to watch out for took place and they were then very upset with him and broke into his car and stole company materials.

At this point Herman left the company due to the theft of company property and the damage to his car and returned home and lived off the software development for almost a year until he was called back to work for the Electrical company who needed him to supervise some new installations for the oil refineries.

© Herman R. Willett

Returning to Electrical Installations

In 1987 Herman was working as the lead electrician over a system upgrade at a refinery in south Texas. One day he simply needed a drink and left his group and walked up the road to the Engineering office where the water fountain was located and walked inside and got a cup of water.

While he was standing there drinking he noticed two of the engineers working on a kaypro 2 computer. They had a chip out looking at it. One of them turned and noticed Herman standing there and said, "Hey, Herman, you like fooling with computers and electronics, do you think you could find the pine out of this chip for us and let us know tomorrow."

Herman said, "Sure, let me see it."

Herman took the chip and looked at it and smiled and grabbed a pin and paper and drew the chip and labeled the parts and named them and handed it to them and simply smiled at them as they looked at him in astonishment and then Herman simply turned and left the building.

Understanding Corporate America

About 30 minutes later the two engineers drove up to where Herman was working with his group and said, "Herman, we have a problem we have been trying to fix for just over 2 years, it is with computers, we would like a new look, would you mind?"

Herman smiled and said, "Sure why not, sounds like fun and I like computers but you guys know that."

The lead engineer said, "Well jump in, we need to go to another facility."

Herman got in the car and rode with them several miles up the road to another complex, one in which he had also worked back in the day and he saw right away the changes that had taken place.

"So what is the problem?" Herman asks as they drive up.

"Well, we have upgraded the orifice plate calculation system and monitoring systems to cyber systems, and they all work well until we stop pumping in or out and then they go crazy, showing flow rates are still active."

Herman thinks for a moment and then says, "Have you checked the orifice plate systems to see if the differentials are working properly?"

They both look at each other and smile and say, "Yes, of course."

Herman then says, "Well let me look at them and see what I can find."

For two days Herman looks at all the orifice plates as well as sensors and cannot find nothing wrong. So he goes to the engineers and says, "It has to be an engineering or software problem with the cyber system."

Both engineers look at each other and the older one says, "That is what we have thought also and so we mentioned it to the company that built the systems and the software, they have checked it out also, but can find no problems with it."

Herman thinks a bit and says, "Well, can I look at the computer system and the software, a new set of eyes?"

Both engineers look at each other and they say, "Why not, it's worth a try."

A few days later Herman is met by the engineers and they say that the company and corporate has agreed to him looking at the software but has to wait for the people who designed the system to be present. Herman agrees and a few days later they arrive and Herman returns to the system.

Understanding Corporate America

© Herman R. Willett

They system is a series of tall Unix towers that ran the system, Herman is give access to them and he looks into them and in about an hour finds a problem and fixes it.

He finds the problem and tells the engineers and the people from the refinery that are present what he has found at that a simple basic mathematic formula would fix it.

"You are taking the square root of the flow rate, but even when there is no flow." Herman says. "Make it stop if it is less than 1 but greater than 0, that is what I did."

The group look at him like he is crazy and then the engineer he has been working with says, "Oh yea, basic math. The orifice plates still show flow rates a little and since it is less than zero it looks like it is flowing faster to the sensors."

Everyone looks stunned and then looks at Herman. A week later he was working for one of the biggest oil companies in the world, especially after all the problems were not eliminated by the flow rate measurement system.

Understanding Corporate America
© Herman R. Willett

Working for Corporate America

Herman went to work for the big oil company as one if the primary system engineers for the cyber system division and was place in charge of building and installing the new systems to run the refineries.

During the first year there was a big union strike and Herman had to be relocated to a secrete hidden bunker area to build the cyber systems due to safety protocols, but eventually her retuned to the refinery were they were installing the systems.

Over time the systems were installed and the fiber optic systems that controlled them were also installed.

During this time also Herman reprogrammed a lot of older systems and networked them together and had them doing things that were impossible according to the computer people with doctorates in computer science and engineering at the time.

Then the corporate meeting took place and the first big lesson that Herman learned came about, one that almost cost him his perfect job and would have if they would have had someone to replace him at the time.

Understanding Corporate America

Herman did not know at the time that his job was in jeopardy and only his experience and understanding of things and how they actually worked and his ability to create new solutions from scratch is what saved his job with the company at this time.

© Herman R. Willett

A Big Mistake

On December 14, 1991 Herman was called to the refinery managers office on the third floor of the main office building for a meeting to discuss his plans for the cyber systems for the entire refinery upgrade. He did not know who the other people attending were so made a big mistake.

Herman was supposed to make his presentation about the next phases of the cyber systems engineering division and the planed to move the refinery forward into the cyber division after the meeting with the rest of the people was completed.

As Herman sat and listened to the people talk as usual he opened his mouth and started pointing out mistakes and ramifications of their actions. The short cuts to save on money and get things done faster were going to cause a lot of problems as well as expand the cost of completing the job correctly so Herman made the mistake of opening his mouth and speaking up.

Both Herman's boss who was at the meeting and the refinery manager looked at him with a shocked expression on their faces while the other people in the room looked at him like he had no idea what he was even talking about.

"Do you know who the f... I am?" One of the high up people shouted at him.

Herman not knowing simply said, "No I do not, we have never met before."

The man shouted, "I am the senior corporate engineer that is designing and managing these projects and you some low down worker thinks he knows more than I do about this."

Herman just looked at him and said, "I did not know, I was just pointing...."

The man yelled back at Herman and said, "Well perhaps you just need to shut your mouth and learn from the experts."

At that point Herman looked at his boss who was shaking his head and looking down at the table. About that time the refinery manager spoke up and said, "Herman, write down everything you say will happen, and listen to them talk and write down any issues you may come up with and give them to me when our meeting is over, ok."

Understanding Corporate America

"Yes sir." Herman responded and proceeded to do so and when it was his time to speak he toke them his plans for the cyber systems division and totally confused the computer experts present for the meeting.

Understanding Corporate America
© Herman R. Willett

Moving from Manager to Supervisor

Over the next year Herman continued to do his project as well as the other people doing theirs. Then in 1992 Herman is called into the refinery managers office where two if the people from the meeting the year before were present.

"Sit down Herman." The refinery manager says.

Herman sits down and looks at them wondering what is going on as the refinery manager goes through paperwork and then looks at Herman and says, "You know Herman, every one of the things you said was going to happen did happen just exactly as you said. How did you know this when these people are highly educated?"

Herman looks at the manager and then at the two engineers and says, "May I ask the engineers a couple questions in order for you to get your answer?"

"Sure, go ahead." The refinery manager tells Herman.

Herman looks at the two men and asks, "You both graduated at the top of your class and have your degrees, right?"

Both men respond with a yes, and Herman then asks, "How many of these actual installations and designs have you personally did yourself other than in the class room?"

Both men look at each other and then respond, "We designed them, we don't build and install them, that is for the construction people to do."

"So, you know how to do it without actually doing it and understanding it, that is the difference between you and me, I learned by doing, not by class room only education."

At that point the refinery manager looked at Herman and said, "Mr. Willett, I am giving you a promotion to Supervisor over our local Cyber Systems Division, not just the engineer.

For the next year Herman worked as the Cyber Systems Division, which also included a lot of plane flights.

Understanding Corporate America
© Herman R. Willett

Living on Air Plaines

After being promoted to Supervisor, a lot of other changes took place, including the need for being officially educated so the company paid to get Herman his degrees in the fields he was already an expert in, which make a lot of time on the air plains.

And then the next event took place. The company had hired a lot of fresh out of collage cyber system graduates that had graduated at the top of their classes to build the same systems for all the refineries that Herman had build for the one he worked at but there was problems, they could not get the systems to work properly and the coding was confusing to them. So Herman started living on airplanes, flying out on Monday and back on Friday every two weeks to see his family over the weekend.

For the next year Herman spent weeks at a time flying to Fairfax, VA to teach the post graduates how to program by showing them how to blend electronics and cyber systems together.

Understanding Corporate America

The problem was that they had mastered their programming and computer science skills but did not comprehend the electrical and electronic aspects of the cyber systems.

In order to do the job properly you had to be a programmer, a computer engineer, an electrical engineer and electronics engineer all at the same time.

Over the next year Herman educated these postgraduates on how to accomplish such goals and again moved up within the company.

Eventually the education was completed and Herman was allowed to return to his home and only fly out from time to time when needed but he did get a major promotion to Regional Supervisor for the company.

Understanding Corporate America
© Herman R. Willett

Moving from Supervisor to Regional

In June of 1996 Herman got promoted to Regional Supervisor of the Cyber Systems Division for the company. It was at this point that some major education took place, not in the technical or engineering or even management perspectives, but the start of Corporate expectations and a whole new comprehension of how Corporate level people thought.

One day Herman was sitting in his office when his supervisor from corporate walked in unannounced.

"Hey Jorge." Herman says standing and shaking his hand. Jorge shakes it back and looked kind of confused and then he smiles and says, "Well, you have not been educated on corporate level yet, but that is also why I am here."

Herman watches as Jorge lays a small folder down on the desktop and then looks at him before continuing. "I am here to go over a few things with you, now that you are a supervisor, there are some corporate guidelines that I need to make you aware of. Normally, or I should say almost never is a person promoted to supervisor from as low as you were when you came in, in fact most supervisors and above never serve such low levels because it interferes with their ability to do their job correctly.'

Herman looks at Jorge for a moment not knowing what to say or how to respond and Jorge smiles and says, "This is your file of all the things that have been put in for you during the time you have worked for the company, go ahead and open it and look at it."

Herman opens the file and looks at it and after a minute says, "I have 4 right ups for bad things but not one good thing for all the work over the years, and the write ups are stupid."

Jorge smiles and says, "Well this is your first education, as a supervisor you have to write up each of your employees with at least one negative thing each year, you have to find something, like in yours."

Herman looks at his file again and says, "The dirty shoes in the dining room was because of the flood in the kitchen that me and another person rushed in to fix."

"Yes, but you walked back out of the kitchen into the dining area with dirty shoes. So you got rote up for it, that was how your

© Herman R. Willett

boss was able to find one thing that year for you to be written up for."

"What if I can not find anything to write someone up for, I understand you are telling me that my file here is an example of what I have to do as a supervisor."

"Yes, that is correct, you have to find at least one thing to write them up for each year."

"Why?" Herman asks, "What if they are my best people that I have no problems with and they do the best jobs?"

Jorge looks at Herman and says, "That is the biggest problem, and the ones that need to be wrote up the most and also the ones you need to have the most face to face talks with to keep them under control."

Herman looks at him and then understands why he had so many face-to-face talks about things with his boss and smiles and then says, "So, what about the ones that I have problems with that I can not depend on, do I treat them less?"

Jorge smiles and says, "Correct, they are easy to control and we don't need to keep them in the watch so to speak, but the people that do their job without problems and do it well we need to keep them in fear of their job and also keep writing the up at least once per year and keep it in their file in case we need it in the future."

"Need it in the future?" Herman asks puzzled.

"Yes, so we can terminate their employment and have a valid legal means.

"So we cook the books so to speak." Herman responds.

"Well, that is corporate America, Herman. More concerned about keeping cost low and production high to make the money and just replace people who don't agree, it's not about doing the job right, but getting the job done with the lowest cost and most prophet."

Herman shakes his head and says, "That is just not right, that is so wrong that I don't even thing the devil world agree with it."

"Well Herman, I guess it is your turn to be the devil. Read this booklet and follow it." Jorge says and stands up and heads to the door, then pauses and says, "I'll talk to you next week at home office, bring in your reports on your employees and have a bad thing for each of them listed."

Understanding Corporate America
© Herman R. Willett

After Herman's boss leaves he looks at the documents listed and also the files of each of his workers and the notes left by the former Supervisor and becomes very angry at how unjust and inappropriate and unethical they system is.

On the trip to corporate Herman put in the files that he witnessed one walking with damaged shoos, another with a ripped pants and several others without their protective gear or name badges. And he was told he needed to find at least one more thing for each that could be held against them as these could not hold up.

The lessons on corporate mentality had started and it was apparent that Corporate had not one concept of reality, only money money money, and not one sign of ethics or proper conduct outside of greed.

Herman sat and thought about it for a long time before continuing his job. He loved the computer management and oversight position where he could make sure things were done correctly instead of by the book directives but hated the position he was put in to micro manage. For he understood micromanagement is a position from hell and people that feel that they have to micromanage are often failures.

But the lessons in Micromanagement were just beginning for both Herman and the corporation. Herman learned more and more and the corporation(s) eventually learned from Herman also as well as others that Herman was able to get to comprehend reality vs. Micromanagement income creation.

© Herman R. Willett

Moving from Regional to Cyber Systems Administrator

In March of 1997, Herman was promoted to corporate level Cyber Systems Administrator and given the job of overseeing the cyber systems for the United States for the company.

This was also another major turning point in Herman's life and another point at which he had another wake up call about the concepts of Corporate America and Corporations in general and how the people who ran them really and truly had no concept of the reality of the job and the reality of the every day world that they ran from the corporate level.

In the end both Herman and the corporation learned from each other many things. Herman learned that it was all about money for the companies and not about what really was important or what was really safe for the work environment and the corporation learned that they were actually costing themselves money in the end due to not understanding the essentials.

This caused a problem and a solution in which Herman was able to instruct and get instructed and in the end became understanding of corporate perspectives.

Understanding Corporate America

The first thing that they wanted Herman to do when he was promoted was make a trip to the corporate head quarters to meet with corporate people face to face to become "educated" on proper procedures. The flight was taken and the lessons were learned, and a new understanding of the reality of Corporations came about for Herman.

Understanding Corporate America

Going to Corporate

On the flight to home office Herman read the manuals and directives that would be reviewed in the paper work sent him before he left his home base. The information was totally confusing and he had many questions to ask when he got there.

One of the main things was that in order for the company to be functional it had to have large incomes and to do that costs had to be kept to a minimum and hours had to be kept to a minimum for the workers but the work had to be completed on time.

Reading the paperwork and the directives of his new position started to really affect Herman in an ethical way. Being a person with sound and strong moral ethics he was starting to wonder if he could even do the job, but decided since he was going to be over the cyber systems division there would not be much need for the terrorist techniques, as he called them, to be used against his staff.

Understanding Corporate America

After getting off the airplane and going and checking into his hotel, Herman took a quick look around Washington DC before heading on the drive to the corporate office of the company.

When he arrived the lessons started all over and only got more confusing and impractical but the understanding of how an what corporate America was and what corporations actually were came to comprehension better than any other way possible.

Understanding Corporate America
© Herman R. Willett

First Lessons in Corporate Concept of Reality

When Herman made it to the corporate head quarters that afternoon for his first meeting the instant lessons were shocking.

Walking into the building Herman asked which way he needed to go to get to the meeting and ended up on an elevator with three other people all corporate level.

While listening to the conversation it was all he could do to keep his mouth shut.

"It is only a 600 foot length, I don't know why that stupid electrician thinks that we need to use a larger cable, it is just running a single device and we have tested them at the test facility and it runs great with the 12 gage wiring there."

"We know, we had our test facility retest the cabling and equipment again for a full month with no problems, so we don't need the 8 gage wire, the 12 will work just fine."

Herman listening to them had several big questions to ask if they had considered but instead kept his mouth shut knowing exactly what the electrician they were talking about was concerned with but remained silent.

Understanding Corporate America

As he got off the elevator, Herman also knew that in the end these people would not be at fault he had heard talking on the elevator would not be at fault and the company would blame the contractor or electrician for the issues and cause them to end up paying for repairs or take the blame and get a bad reputation and not be used again when in fact if the men had listened to them problems and extra costs could have been avoided.

With this on his mind Herman went on to the meeting and was greeted by a couple of people he knew, one being his former supervisor which now was his equal within the company.

When the meeting started, the senior corporate person stood up and walked over to Herman and said point blankly, "We normally do not promote from the bottom up to such a level as this due to the problems it creates, but Mr. Willett, we had no choice in this matter and welcome to Corporate Perspectives for the company. I hope you can grasp what we are about to teach you.

The man then simply turned and walked away to start addressing the entire group present for the talk.

Understanding Corporate America

During the meeting Herman listened to the presentations and discussions and was flabbergasted at what was talked about.

One of the first things that got his attention was the discussion about cutting back on costs by going with a contractor that was a little bit more expensive than another but said he could do the same job with less expensive equipment and still come out father under budget that the lower cost contractor.

When Herman heard what was being done the first thing that came to mind was the dangers involved with going with the other equipment and the extra cost it would create in the end. He remained silent but apparently the look on his face got the attention of others.

"Mr. Willett, do you have a comment?" The corporate level person asked.

Herman looked over at his former supervisor who gave him the silent look and Herman said in response, "No sir, just trying to follow your reasoning."

The corporate level man looked confused and finally aid, "Money, Mr. Willett, Money. Yes we have enough to pay the most expensive and still have a profit, but infesters need more income."

Understanding Corporate America

Herman looked at the man and wanted to ask, "How can doing this give them more money when in the end it will cost them money." But instead remained silent for a moment and responded, "I am learning sir, just a different perspective is all."

The corporate person looked at Herman and said, "I am glad, but I can tell you have issues with this, can you explain them to me so we can have a record?"

Herman hesitated and the corporate person spoke up again saying, "It will not be held against you, we just want them on file so that in the future we can show them to you and teach you where you were at fault."

Herman smiled internally at that point and understood that their objective would in the end back fire on them so opened his mouth and spoke up. "Sir, you are talking about a difference in wiring length here. In your test facility you have the exact same equipment but at a shorter feed level so yes they will work just fine. However at the feed level you indicated here the current restrictions involved will cause a failure and over load and possible circuit fracturing. In the end it will fail, sir."

Understanding Corporate America
© Herman R. Willett

The men looked at Herman like he was talking a foreign language to them and asked to explain it in more detail which he did and it still left them confused and in the end the main person said, "Mr. Willett, we have it under good authority that what you tell us will not happen."

Herman smiled and remained silent as the conversation went on to other matters.

A few moths later Herman got a call at his office at the refinery where he worked from the corporate person that had told him that they had good authority that nothing would happen and he apologized and asked him to return to corporate to discuss how he knew things would happen.

The trip was made and people listened to him as he explained the science and physics of things and focused on that instead of money money money. In the end they came to understand that focusing on money and income as the primary goal would in the end cost them more than it would to spend a little more up front and have more income, or as they said it, "positive feed".

Understanding Corporate America

Over the next several months both Herman and Corporate level people learned form each other. Herman learned more and more about the corporate level comprehensions of reality and that it was about income as a primary and less about doing thing correctly as the other objective. It was a big eye-opening event for Herman but only the beginning.

© Herman R. Willett

Health Issues

Then another life changing event happened in September of 1997. Herman had taken several flights the past few weeks and then had driven to Memphis from south Texas to visit his wife and daughter who where in the RV at the Graceland RV Park. They had decided to stay another month so Herman drove home to fly out that Monday morning to the corporate head quarters.

However when Herman got out of bed that morning a dizzy spell got him and he fell to the floor unconscious. After waking up he got ready to drive to the refinery to prepare for his flight out that Monday morning, but it was never made. He woke up three days later in the hospital with his son sitting beside him who had drove in from three states away.

It took three years for his health to get to the point where he could function again and at that point he reopened Dynamic Software Solutions and started installing Internet into hotels and apartment complexes as well as businesses in South Texas. But the income was not enough to pay for housing as well as the new medical costs.

Understanding Corporate America

Belinda, Herman's wife went to work for a convenience store as the night manager and worked with them for several years until she was offered a job at Graceland in Memphis at which time they moved to Memphis and Herman continued the monitoring and control of the hotels and apartment complexes and retirement homes. Life was good, but then more economic hard ships came about, the cost of Herman's medicine was more then they could afford, so Herman started looking for Computer Jobs or even simple IT or programming jobs and had an interview for one, at least he thought that was what it was for.

In the end it was another bottom up to corporate level thing that educated him even more on corporate level perspectives.

Understanding Corporate America

Moving to Insurance Sells

When Herman arrived at the interview it was not for a computer position but for insurance sells. Well since they were offering us a free meal Herman decided to sit and listen to them since the meal would cover the cost of the drive.

During the time listening to them he realized that if he had had the kind of insurance coverage that they offered when he got sick he would still be covered and there would have been no spike in premiums due to his illness. Wondering where this kind of insurance had been when he needed it, he decided it was something he wanted to do in order to help people so he signed up to become an insurance agent.

After several months of training he was certified and licensed in four states to do Insurance cells and started a new corer but also a new understanding. Some of the previous corporate level understanding helped him make decisions that helped out but also was against corporate policy. However just like at the refinery, these decisions moved him up the ranks with the company.

© Herman R. Willett

Sales and Marketing

The main problem with the health insurance industry and when he went to work was that the insurance agents were in it for the money and not to help the people who wanted affordable health insurance.

Working with various people and following corporate guidelines was generating income for the company but also hurting our customers. They were being sold policies by the agents (the agents that were at fault) that give them affordable insurance but also cost them more money up front and for basic medical issues with the affordable part being when major illnesses took place and they had no out of pocket costs.

After looking at things Herman realized that yes what he was selling helped people and made the company large amounts of prophet for the investors but it bothered me that it was taking away from what the people needed, truly affordable health insurance.

Additionally the marketing guidelines presented by the company and that we had to follow was pushing more people away than bringing them in and the quick cancellations of policies was another problem.

Understanding Corporate America

Following Corporate Guidelines

One of the biggest things to over come was the daily call numbers you had to make to set up meetings with people. Corporate had a list of names to call as well as taking inbound calls and setting up the home visits or the office visits. There was strict guidelines to follow and which products to market.

After about six months on the job Herman was doing ok but out of the 60 insurance agents in his region with the company he was number 58 in production and sells, the policies he sold were the highest income ones for the company but also the ones that he found out were being dropped within in a couple months.

He called one of his customers one day and asked why the policy had been dropped and she told him that it was to expensive, yes the price was low and affordable but when she went to the hospital she had to pay a lot out of pocket and if she had went into the hospital she would not have had to pay anything just like he had told her.

It was at this point that he understood a major thing; the company was more concerned with the profit potential than the health and wellness of the customers.

Understanding Corporate America
© Herman R. Willett

It was at this point that Herman decided to do the ethical and morally correct thing and treat his customers as he would want to be treated since he was unable to get insurance himself, he wanted to make sure that his customers did not end up like him.

So he decided to do what was right for the customers and what was ethically right across the board, and started listening to customers and selling them what they wanted instead of pushing the ones that the corporation wanted him to do so that they could make more prophet. In the end his actions caused more customers to stay with the company and raised the prophet margins in his region. This lead to a promotion and a call to corporate in order to educate corporate level people on the reality of things, a repeat of the previous events with the refinery.

During the meeting with corporate Herman was asked how he went from low to the 4th highest producer in his region as well as how he was keeping clients for over a year when the others were dropping their policies after a few months. The answer stunned and shocked and educated Corporate and he was asked to teach others how to do the same.

Understanding Corporate America

Making a Decision to Do unto Others

During the corporate level discussion Herman was asked to explain how he accomplished the high level of sales and retention so he agreed to attend a corporate meeting to explain it.

When he was introduced Herman took the microphone and said, "Do unto others as you would have them do unto you." He then paused and said, "I am sure you all have heard this, but do you understand it? It simply means to treat other people, as you would want to be treated. So let me ask you this, would you want to be sold a bill of goods that made the seller a lot of profit while at the same time left you in need of more or would you want a bill of goods that helped you and the seller? Which would be more beneficial to you both, high profit from the sell to you and you being in need an having to spend more money and canceling and causing the seller to loose money or purchase a cheaper better plan that made the seller less money up front but over the long rune larger profits. What is more important, profit or taking care of people? What is more important, that dollar or the life of the person.

Understanding Corporate America

Can you kill someone to make a dollar or would you give up a dollar to safe a life and still have a dollar left over. What is more important, 2 dollars and a dead person or 1 dollar and a live person. That is all I am asking you to think about, which is more important, profit or the human life and the ability of the person to live a good and happy life."

When Herman finished speaking he looked around the room and a lot of the people there were looking down at the tables and a few were crying and yet a few more were shaking there heads and pointing at him as if they were disgusted with what he had to say.

The executive of the company then walked over to Herman and shook his head with tears in his eyes and said, "Mr. Willett, that was a good talk, it got the point across to me. You may sit down."

Herman then went and sat down while the executive officer stood wiping his eyes and then he said, "I have been in upper management my entire life it seems, but I have never had my heart touch in such a way as today. Yes we are an investment company today, not like we were in the past, but as Mr. Willett said, we are here for the people.

© Herman R. Willett

He paused and then said, "I have to admit, the company needs prophet due to investments but what is more important, we are an insurance company that helps people afford their medical costs, that should be our primary focus."

He then looks over at Herman and says, "Mr. Willett, thank you for opening my eyes, I will talk to your supervisor and you can have the promotion and your own region, the North West Arkansas region and the state of Arkansas if you so desire."

Herman was speechless as he sat there contemplating what was just said and offered to him.

Herman was given the Northwest Arkansas region and became the lead insurance producer in that area for just a few months. Over those few months he sold quiet a few low income policies that made the company a lot of money and his customers kept them long term.

But what caused Herman to leave the company was not lack of accomplishment but the offer of a better paying job and now since he had got the company to understand what was important, that it was the customer and their health and not profit, he felt safe doing so.

Understanding Corporate America
© Herman R. Willett

While looking for a place to live, the apartment complex that Belinda was applying for offered them both a job as potential managers based upon their backgrounds, so it was taken and within six weeks they were made managers of an apartment complex for 5 years.

Yet again more corporate type lessons were learned.

Understanding Corporate America

The Promotion

After training for six weeks under the managers currently at the apartment complex and seeing how simple it was compared to both of their previous experiences, it was an easy thing to do and less stressful.

With in that six-week period they actually co-managed the complex with the current managers and then the supervisor said it was time to move Herman and Belinda up and promoted them to Managers and moved the current managers to a larger complex to take over.

Becoming a Property Manager

Becoming the property manager was easy, the only problem was Herman was the maintenance person as well as the property manager as there was not one on staff. But it was good.

Also there was no sells and marketing to be done as that went directly through home office, the only sales that took place was when people called in or walked in looking for an apartment.

Since there were no outbound sales calls to be done, life as a property manager was easy and their community stayed full till the financial collapse, and at that point the managers got blamed for empty apartments.

Understanding Corporate America

© Herman R. Willett

Following Corporate Guidelines Again

It was interesting to watch the corporate level aspect come back, "if your apartments are empty it must be because you are not doing your job right." Was the message that everyone was receiving, Herman and Belinda talked to supervisors about it and all they were told was to "get people in." Well it was hard to do so if no one was walking in looking for apartments to rent. But this was something that corporate America did not comprehend.

So the jiff came down that if you did not rent apartments your job was in jeopardy, but then all across the company it was happening so eventually it came to be understood at upper management levels that it was indeed not manager's faults.

Herman recognized the scare tactics again and understood that corporate had made the big mistake of blaming the lower down for things that they had no control over no matter what. Luckily the across the country economic collapse help Corporate understand.

However corporate did come up with a concept that helped rent apartments but it lowered their profit margins quiet a bit.

But they were able to understand that some positive profit was better than a lot of negative loss, and things progressed.

Herman and Belinda stayed with the company as managers until Herman's health kicked in again and he was found unconscious laying on the ground at the apartment complex and then a short while later had a seizure in front of one of the corporate people.

They allowed them both to step down and stay with the company, currently Herman is on medical leave and Belinda is working as a senior leasing agent with the company at another complex. The company has been gracious and thankful enough to give them a free apartment to live in and work to have some income. Herman still runs his Dynamic Software Solutions business that he has had for over 30 years and that helps also.

But now lets look at how to handle corporate America now that you understand the author's background and perspectives.

Doing the Right Thing

One of the hardest things that were learned by me, Herman R. Willett, the author of this book, over the years is that America and Civilization has lost a lot of ethics. It seems that it is all about the might dollar instead of what is important.

Just stop and ask yourself, if you were in need would you want someone to help you or not do so because it would cost them money or reduce their profit margins.

Now put yourself in their shows after thinking about you being the one in need and if you saw someone in need and you could help them by giving up a little bit of income and staying financially above board, what would you do.

Would you help that other person (yourself from before) or would you let them suffer (yourself from before)?

Humanity today is going down hill because it is all about money and profits and such instead of what is important. Yes unfortunately we need and depend on money to survive which in my opinion is something that should not be.

Understanding Corporate America
© Herman R. Willett

Yes un-necessary items should be something a business can do, but necessary things should never have to depend on money.

Sometime you just have to do what is right even though society and the upper level people think it is wrong or say not to do so, for in the end it is you that will have to answer for your deeds and not them.

Choose to follow the evil or the righteous, it is your choice; you can choose to do good or do bad, but always remember in the end what good is money and power if you have no conscious or essence of right and wrong.

Do unto others as you would have them do unto you, treat others as you would want to be traded. If you are a high up person in a corporation, don't ignore that fact that the people down below are just as much human as you are and are privilege to the exact same rights and life as you are. For when you put money and power over humanity and human decency you have lost you way and are nothing more than the devils angel so to speak.

Always remember that what we do to others will always come back to us, if you punish for profit, you will be punished also, just a different kind of pain and suffering.

Understanding Corporate America

© Herman R. Willett

Becoming Successful

Over time I have always become successful and that is the main strike of this book, but not everyone will be or can be as lucky was I was, growing up in a time when geeks were needed and corporations had to do what needed to be done.

But also, it was a lesson of extreme learning protocols that helped me understand the mindsets of corporate America and the downfall of our society that it is creating.

The next, last and final chapter will go over these lessons in detail so that you can understand the corporate perspective in your work place and know that you are not at fault, you are only being made to think you are as a type of intimidation.

And good people are often fired or demoted just to keep the fear factor working strongly so that you are subjugated and controlled instead of recognized and rewarded for your efforts.

Understanding Corporate America
© Herman R. Willett

Corporate America and the Ignorance it creates

So what are the lessons learned here about the working class and the corporate class? Is it class warfare as some people say or is it simply indifference, or is it just simply ignorance on the part of the higher up.

Well it is a bit of all of the above, and that is what my story here was supposed to point out, but now lets look at the lesson in detail.

Over the years my ability to move up from the bottom to corporate level has been very educational. The most amazing educational experience is that the people in charge at corporate levels have no clue as to what goes own down below and don't want to know. And the reason I have been told many times by corporate level people including senior executives and CEO's of the company is that if they did understand then they would not be able to do their job properly.

Also the fear that can be used that someone can loose their job is a very good thing to use to make more money and if someone leaves or gets fired they just replace them, as it is not quality of work that is important but profit to the corporation.

Understanding Corporate America

© Herman R. Willett

In the end it is all about profit and not about what is right. So it is up to the individuals, weather at corporate level or and the low end to take the personal responsible and use ethics and understanding to do unto the other person as you would want to be treated in the same situation.

Understanding Corporate America

Moving Forward

In the end now, since my health issues have caused many problems, it looks like I will be working from home doing my cyber systems things with my customers around the country while Belinda works at the office here in our new apartment complex where we now live. But it is moving forward, and some day we hope that America will move forward and the concept of corporate greed will go away.

Corporations are a good thing as long as they do what is right and moral and do not simply focus on money. Would you rater be a paramedic and save a life or a thief and take a life because it brought you more money.

Just think of it that way my friends, for some day we will all face that final question at life's end and can we look back and die knowing that we did the right thing to our fellow man.

ISBN 978-1-105-62439-1

9 781105 624391   90000

www.ingramcontent.com/pod-product-compliance
Lightning Source LLC
Chambersburg PA
CBHW021909170526
45157CB00005B/2027